NO BULL REVIEW:

MACROECONOMICS AND MICROECONOMICS

Top Ten Guide

For use with the AP® Macroeconomics and
AP® Microeconomics Exams

CRAIG MEDICO

Table of Contents
No Bull Unit Review

The No Bull Approach (2015 Edition)

No Bull Review..."because your review book, shouldn't need a review book!"

This No Bull Review Top Ten Guide is the most concise and to the point review that you will find for the AP® Macroeconomics and AP® Microeconomics Exams. Our goal here is to give you everything you need to know for class and standardized testing. Sometimes review books can be full of material that you just don't need to know. Or, they give explanations that are just as long as the ones found in the textbooks. The No Bull approach is to cut through the fat, and give you what you want.

We, as authors of No Bull Review, are teachers. For years, we have been speaking to students to find out what you want in a review book. The answer? No Bull. You want the facts, clear and to the point.

Each No Bull Unit Review chapter contains the 10 most important concepts, including all of the necessary graphs and diagrams that you need to know. The first six chapters cover Macroeconomics and the final five chapters recap the main ideas of Microeconomics. Please note that the first chapter on Basic Concepts is required for both, Macroeconomics and Microeconomics, exams.

Remember, this is a no-nonsense study guide designed to maximize your study time. We hope you enjoy the No Bull approach. Thank you, and best of luck!

-No Bull Review

About the author:

Craig Medico is an Economics and History teacher in New York with more than 11 years of classroom experience. He is the developer of several best-selling iPhone test prep apps from Study By App, LLC that are available on iTunes. Visit Mr. Medico's homepage at MrMedico.info for No Bull Review video lessons and other free educational resources.

NB1. Basic Concepts (Macro/Micro)

#1. What is scarcity?

Scarcity is an economic problem resulting from the limited nature of **economic resources** (factors of production). The scarce economic resources are land (natural resources), labor, capital (tools, machines, factories), and entrepreneurship. Every society must determine how it will allocate these scarce economic resources. In **market economies**, markets (supply and demand) allocate resources. Central planners allocate resources in **command economies**, and tribal chiefs and customs allocate resources in **traditional economies**.

#2. What is an opportunity cost?

An **opportunity cost** is the next best alternative for whatever one is doing at the moment. For example, you chose to read this study guide. This is the best activity for you at the moment. If you had something better to do, you would be doing it! Your opportunity cost is the other activity that you are giving up. Buyers and sellers make choices all the time, and these choices come with opportunity costs. For example, choosing to purchase a boat could mean sacrificing the purchase of a new car.

#3. What are the assumptions of the production possibilities curve?

The **production possibilities model** illustrates opportunity costs graphically. In this simplified model, we make the following assumptions:

1. Only two goods are produced by an economy
2. Resources are fixed
3. Technology is fixed
4. Full employment exists on the curve
5. Productive efficiency (producing at lowest cost) occurs on the curve
6. Cannot produce beyond the curve in the present
7. Production inside the curve indicates that there

are unemployed resources

#4. What is the law of increasing opportunity cost?

The **law of increasing opportunity cost** applies to a production possibilities curve (PPC) that is bowed outward from the origin. For an economy to produce more of one good, it must sacrifice increasing quantities of the other good.

PPC: Increasing Opportunity Cost

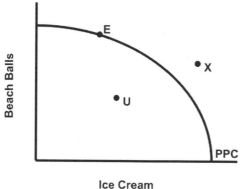

Ice Cream

The PPC above depicts increasing opportunity costs. Point *U* represents unemployment, point *E* represents full employment and productive efficiency, and point *X* represents a point that is unattainable at the moment.

If opportunity costs are constant, then the PPC is a straight line. This means that the economic resources are perfect substitutes in the production of the two goods.

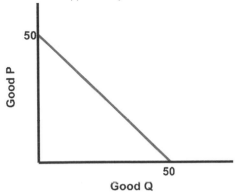

PPC: Constant Opportunity Cost

#5. How do you determine absolute advantage and comparative advantage?

To determine which country or economy has the **absolute advantage** in the production of a good, you simply look to see which country can produce more. If Nobully can produce 120 yak skin coats and Medicoa can only produce 60 yak skin coats, then Nobully has the absolute advantage in yak skin coats.

You can also determine absolute advantage by seeing which country can produce one unit faster or one unit with the least amount of economic resources.

To determine which country has the **comparative advantage** in the production of a good, you must determine which country has the lowest opportunity cost (smallest sacrifice) in producing the good.

For example: If Nobully can produce 120 yak skin coats or 60 glockenspiels, then its opportunity cost of producing 1 yak skin coat is 1/2 glockenspiel (60 glockenspiels divided by 120 yak skin coats). If Medicoa can produce 60 yak skin coats or 120 glockenspiels, its opportunity cost of 1 yak skin coat is 2 glockenspiels (120 glockenspiels divided by 60 yak skin coats). Nobully has the comparative advantage in yak skin coat production because its opportunity cost (1/2 glockenspiel) is less than Medicoa's opportunity cost (2 glockenspiels).

7

The country with the lower relative opportunity cost of production will specialize in the production of that good and then export that good if trade occurs. Nobully should specialize in yak skin coats and Medicoa should specialize in glockenspiels.

#6. What is the law of diminishing marginal utility?

The **law of diminishing marginal utility** states that as you consume a product, your additional happiness from consuming one more unit falls. For example, you just ate your fourth taco and realize that the third taco gave you more additional satisfaction than the fourth taco. That's because of diminishing marginal utility. Say you just completed your seventh year of marriage, and realize that your additional happiness gained in the seventh year is less than the additional happiness gained in the sixth year. That's because of diminishing marginal utility.

Your **total utility** or total happiness increases as you consume more units of a product, however, the rate that your total utility increases will fall at some point. That is diminishing marginal utility.

Value lies at the margin: Water will give you more total satisfaction throughout your life than the diamonds that you own. However, the marginal utility of the last diamond you purchased is much greater than the last glass of water you drank. That idea along with the concept of scarcity explains why diamonds are very expensive and water is cheap.

#7. How does the law of supply and demand work?

In a **market**, buyers and sellers come together to establish equilibrium prices and quantities of goods and services. The law of supply consists of a direct relationship between price and quantity, and the law of demand consists of an inverse relationship between price and quantity. When the supply and demand curves intersect, market equilibrium is established. Assuming no externalities exist, the intersection of supply and demand is allocatively efficient.

Supply & Demand: Video Game Market in Equilibrium

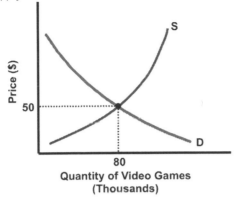

#8. What is the difference between a shortage and a surplus?

A **shortage** occurs in a market when the quantity demanded exceeds the quantity supplied. Assuming no price controls or natural disasters, a shortage is only temporary and market forces will push prices back up toward equilibrium. If the government establishes an effective **price ceiling** (legal maximum price) below the market price, the shortage is long term.

A **surplus** occurs within a market when the quantity supplied exceeds the quantity demanded. Assuming no government price controls, a surplus is temporary and market forces will push the price back down toward equilibrium. If the government establishes an effective **price floor** (legal minimum price) above market price, the surplus is long term.

#9. What causes a shift in the demand and supply curves?

A change in any of the following will cause the **demand curve to shift** to the right (causing market price and quantity to increase) or to the left (causing market price and quantity to decrease):

1. Tastes and preferences
     Example: an increase in popularity of a good will shift demand right
2. Consumer income
     Example: an increase in income will shift demand for a *normal good* right, but an increase in income will shift demand for an *inferior good* right
3. Number of buyers
     Example: an increase in the number of buyers will shift demand right
4. Substitute good's price
     Example: an increase in the price of a substitute good will shift demand right
5. Complementary good's price
     Example: a decrease in the price of a complementary good will shift demand right
6. Expectations of future prices
     Example: an increase in future price expectations will shift demand right

Demand Shifts Right: Price Increases, Quantity Increases

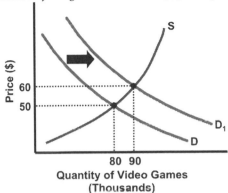

Quantity of Video Games
(Thousands)

A change in any of the following will cause the **supply curve to shift** to the right (causing market price to decrease and quantity to increase) or to the left (causing market price to increase and quantity to decrease):

1. Resource prices
   Example: a decrease in resource prices will shift supply right
2. Technology and productivity
   Example: an increase in labor productivity will shift supply right
3. Number of sellers
   Example: an increase in the number of sellers will shift supply right
4. Subsidies to producers / Taxes on production
   Example: an increase in per-unit subsidies will shift supply right
5. Expectations of future prices
   Example: a decrease in future price expectations will shift supply right
6. Alternative output price changes
   Example: a decrease in the price of a good that uses the same resources will shift supply right

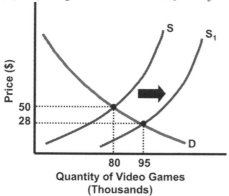

**Quantity of Video Games
(Thousands)**

#10. What happens when supply and demand shift at the same time?

When the supply and demand curves shift at the same time, the change in market price or quantity will be **indeterminate** (increase, decrease, or stay the same). This is assuming that we do NOT know how far each curve will shift.

When supply and demand both increase (shift to the right), the equilibrium quantity will increase, but market price will be indeterminate. When supply and demand both decrease (shift to the left), the equilibrium quantity will decrease, but market price will be indeterminate.

When supply increases and demand decreases, market price will decrease, but equilibrium quantity will be indeterminate. When supply decreases and demand increases, market price will increase, but equilibrium quantity will be indeterminate.

NB2. Economic Performance (Macro)

#1. How does the circular flow model work?

The **circular flow model** is a system of incentives that shows how businesses and households interact through product markets and resource markets. Households demand goods and services from businesses in the product market while businesses supply the goods and services. Businesses demand resources from households in the factor market while households supply the resources.

Circular Flow Model

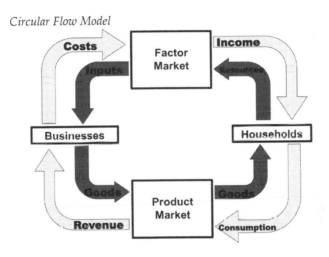

The government can be added to the middle of the diagram since it provides public goods, services, and transfer payments to households and businesses. The government also collects taxes from households and businesses.

#2. What is included in a nation's gross domestic product?

The four components to a nation's **gross domestic product** (GDP) are consumer expenditures (what households buy), gross investment spending (what businesses buy), government spending (what government buys), and net export spending (what we export minus what we import). The GDP accounts for the production of goods and services within a country's borders in one year.

There are three components to **gross investment**:

1. Business investment (capital goods, nonresidential structures, intellectual property)
2. Residential investment (housing)
3. Adjustments to inventories (accounts for unsold goods produced in the current year)

You can add up a nation's overall income to get GDP too. GDP is equal to the sum of wages and salaries, rents, interest income, profits, indirect business taxes, depreciation of capital, and net foreign factor income.

#3. What is excluded from a nation's gross domestic product?

A nation's gross domestic product reflects the production of final goods and services produced legally within a country's borders in one year. The following items are NOT included in the calculation of a country's GDP:

1. Financial transactions (such as stocks & bonds)
2. Transfer payments (such as social security checks)
3. Used goods (such as secondhand golf clubs)
4. Non-market transactions (such as you cleaning your room)
5. Illegal transactions (such as bootlegging)
6. Unreported transactions (such as tips you don't report to the government)
7. Intermediate goods (such as the fabric in your butterfly net)
8. Goods produced in other countries (such as your cellphone)

#4. What is the difference between real GDP and nominal GDP?

Real GDP is output that has been adjusted to hold the price level constant. This way we can measure the level of goods and services that are produced over a period of time without worrying about changes in prices.

Nominal GDP has not been adjusted for changes in the price level and reflects the market value of all goods and services in the year everything was produced.

Real GDP measures all of a nation's output, which makes it one of the most important measurements of economic growth over time. However, an increase in nominal GDP could mean that prices and output have increased; so nominal GDP is NOT the best measurement of growth.

Real GDP = Nominal GDP / GDP Price Index

Real GDP per capita is another great way to measure economic growth and a nation's general economic well being. It represents the output per person within an economy. We use this measure to determine whether a nation's standard of living is increasing or decreasing.

Real GDP Per Capita = Real GDP / Population

#5. What is a business cycle?

The **business cycle** shows the upturns and downturns of economic activity in a nation. It contains four key parts:

1. Expansions (real GDP rises, price level rises, and unemployment rate falls)
2. Peaks (real GDP is at its max and resources are fully employed)
3. Contractions (real GDP falls, price level falls, and unemployment rises)
4. Troughs (real GDP is at its lowest point and unemployment is near its highest point)

This diagram illustrates the four parts along with an upward sloping line to demonstrate the long-term trend of economic growth.

Business Cycle: Expansion, Peak, Contraction, & Trough

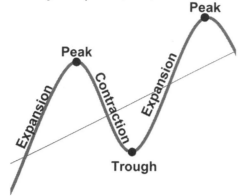

#6. How do you measure the rate of unemployment?

The **unemployment rate** measures the percentage of people in the labor force that are presently unemployed and actively looking for employment.

To calculate the rate of unemployment, take the number of people that are unemployed and looking for work and divide by the number of people that are working plus the number of people looking for work.

Unemployment Rate = $\dfrac{\text{Quantity Unemployed}}{\text{Quantity Labor Force}}$ X 100

The unemployment rate does NOT count **discouraged workers** (people that have given up their job hunt). As a result, the unemployment rate is often understated. There are three main types of unemployment that make up the unemployment rate:

1. **Frictional unemployment** is temporary or seasonal. This includes recent graduates and

16

people who quit their job to find something better.

2. **Structural unemployment** occurs when certain skills of laborers are no longer needed. This includes people who are replaced by technology or new industries through creative destruction. These people need to retrain or move to find work.

3. **Cyclical unemployment** is the result of a recession. This includes people who are laid off from work because the economy has contracted. It is associated with a downturn in the business cycle.

Frictional unemployment and structural unemployment are completely normal within an economy. These two types of unemployment make up an economy's **natural rate of unemployment**.

#7. What is the difference between demand-pull and cost-push inflation?

Demand-pull inflation is caused by an increase in aggregate demand. This means that buyers are pulling up the general price level of goods and services within an economy.

Cost-push inflation is caused by a decrease in short-run aggregate supply. This means that an increase in production costs (resource prices) have caused an increase in the general price level.

Cost-push inflation is less desirable than demand-pull inflation because cost-push inflation is accompanied by a decrease in output and an increase in unemployment. When inflation and unemployment increase at the same time, the economy experiences **stagflation**.

#8. How do you calculate the inflation rate?

The **inflation rate** measures the percentage increase in consumer prices over a period of time. To calculate the inflation rate, we use a consumer price index (CPI). The consumer price index tracks the prices of goods and services that the typical household buys using a market basket sample (CPI = Market Basket of One Year / Market Basket of a Base Year).

$$\text{Inflation Rate} = \frac{\text{New CPI} - \text{Old CPI}}{\text{Old CPI}} \times 100$$

Prices generally rise over time, but sometimes prices fall. **Deflation** occurs when the inflation rate becomes negative. Be careful not to confuse this concept with disinflation. **Disinflation** is when the rate of inflation slows down.

#9. How do you calculate the real interest rate?

To calculate the real interest rate or nominal interest rate, we can use the Fisher equation. The **real interest rate** accounts for changes in the price level and is very important for businesses interested in investment spending. When real interest rates are low, businesses will increase spending. When real interest rates are high, businesses are less likely to invest.

Real Interest Rate = Nominal Interest Rate – Inflation Rate

Nominal Interest Rate = Real Interest Rate + Inflation Rate

You can determine the percentage change in real income with this equation too!

Real Income % Inc. = Nominal Income % Inc. – Inflation Rate

#10. Who are the winners and losers of unanticipated inflation?

When inflation occurs unexpectedly, some people will benefit and some people will NOT benefit. People that make fixed payments, such as debtors, **gain from sudden inflation** because they pay off debt with cheaper dollars. Assuming that these debtors borrowed at a

18

fixed interest rate, the purchasing power of the loaned money (the principal) has decreased.

People that receive fixed payments, such as creditors who lend at a fixed interest rate, **lose from sudden inflation** because they are receiving cheaper dollars. Therefore, people that earn fixed income will NOT benefit from unanticipated inflation.

NB3. AD/AS & Fiscal Policy (Macro)

#1. How do you graph an economy in long run equilibrium using the aggregate demand and aggregate supply model?

To graph an economy that is in long-run equilibrium, it is convenient to use the **aggregate demand and aggregate supply (AD/AS) model.** This is a model that illustrates an entire economy's total demand (all of the spending) and total supply (all of the producing) of goods and services.

Long-run equilibrium means that the economy is fully employed. The short-run aggregate supply curve, long-run aggregate supply curve, and aggregate demand curve should intersect at the same spot. *Price Level* should be labeled on the y-axis and *Real GDP* should be labeled on the x-axis.

AD/AS: Long-Run Equilibrium

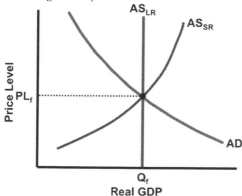

This economy is fully employed and producing at its natural rate of unemployment (zero cyclical unemployment). The **long-run aggregate supply curve** represents the full-employment potential of the economy.

20

#2. How do you graph an economy in recession using the AD/AS model?

To graph an economy experiencing a **recession** in the short run, the aggregate demand curve and short-run aggregate supply curve should intersect to the left of the long-run aggregate supply curve (full-employment level of output).

AD/AS: Recession

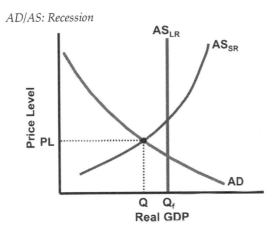

An economy experiences a recession in the short run when the **aggregate demand curve** shifts to the left of the long-run aggregate supply curve. This can be caused by a decrease in consumer spending, investment spending, government spending, and/or net export spending.

#3. How does the economy correct itself from a recession in the long run?

When an economy is in recession in the short run, **classical economic theory** suggests that the government should do nothing (or very little) because the economy will correct itself in the long run.

In the long run, workers will be forced to take nominal wage cuts, as **inflation expectations** and the costs of production fall. The **short-run aggregate supply curve** will shift to the right toward the long-run

21

aggregate supply curve until full employment is restored. The price level will decrease, real GDP will increase, and the unemployment rate will decrease.

#4. How do you graph an economy with high inflation using the AD/AS model?

To graph an economy with high inflation in the short run, the short-run aggregate supply curve and aggregate demand curve should intersect to the right of the long-run aggregate supply curve (full-employment level of output).

AD/AS: Inflation

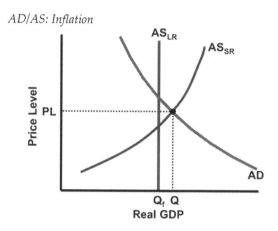

Demand-pull inflation occurs in the short run when the **aggregate demand curve** shifts to the right of the long-run aggregate supply curve. This can be caused by an increase in consumer spending, investment spending, government spending, and/or net export spending.

#5. How will the economy correct itself from high inflation in the long run?

If an economy is experiencing inflation in the short run, **classical economic theory** suggests that the government should do nothing (or very little) because the economy will correct itself in the long run.

22

In the long run, workers will demand higher nominal wages as **inflation expectations rise**. This causes the costs of production to increase. The **short-run aggregate supply curve** will shift to the left toward the long-run aggregate supply curve until the long-run equilibrium is achieved. The price level will increase, real GDP will decrease, and the unemployment rate will increase.

#6. How does fiscal policy affect the federal budget?

Fiscal policy refers to the actions of the government that attempt to shift aggregate demand toward the full-employment level of output in the short run. In **Keynesian economic theory**, the two key tools of fiscal policy are government spending and taxation.

A **budget deficit** occurs when the government spends more than it receives in tax revenue. In this situation, the government must borrow money by issuing new bonds to finance its spending policies. This will increase the **national debt** and lead to the **crowding out effect** (see NB5), two problems associated with expansionary fiscal policies.

A **budget surplus** occurs when the government receives more money in tax revenue than it spends. This helps to reduce the national debt.

#7. How does an expansionary fiscal policy work in the short run?

According to Keynesian economic theory, an **expansionary fiscal policy** is appropriate when the economy is experiencing a recession in the short run. The government can increase spending and/or decrease income taxes to shift aggregate demand to the right. This will increase real GDP, increase the price level, and decrease the unemployment rate.

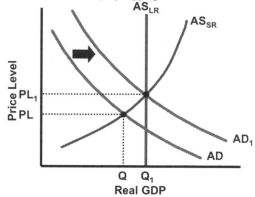

AD/AS: Rightward Shift of Aggregate Demand

When the government passes new legislation to increase spending and/or cut taxes, it is called **discretionary fiscal policy.**

An **automatic stabilizer,** such as a welfare program, goes into effect without the passing of any new laws. During recessions, the government receives less tax revenue and automatically increases certain transfer payments to the private sector.

All of the actions associated with an expansionary fiscal policy will move the federal budget toward a deficit.

#8. How does a contractionary fiscal policy work in the short run?

According to Keynesian economic theory, a **contractionary fiscal policy** is appropriate when the economy is experiencing inflation in the short run. The government can decrease spending and/or increase income taxes to shift aggregate demand to the left. This will decrease real GDP, decrease the price level, and increase the unemployment rate.

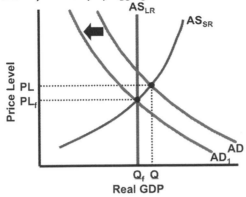

Contractionary fiscal policies move the federal budget balance toward a surplus. This is assuming that tax revenue rises and the government cuts back on its borrowing.

#9. How does the spending multiplier work?

In Keynesian economic theory, the **spending multiplier** is used to determine how much a change in spending will change output. To calculate the spending multiplier, simply divide 1 by the marginal propensity to save (**1/MPS or 1/1-MPC**).

Once you have the spending multiplier, multiply the change in spending by the spending multiplier. This will give you the change in real GDP.

You can use the marginal propensities to determine changes in consumption or savings from a change in **disposable income**. If the marginal propensity to consume (MPC) is 0.8, you will spend 80% of any change in income. If the MPS is 0.2, you will save 20% of any change in income. Because disposable income can only be spent or saved, MPC + MPS = 1.

#10. How does the tax multiplier compare to the spending multiplier?

According to Keynesian economic theory, the tax multiplier is calculated using **–MPC/MPS**. The tax multiplier is less than the spending multiplier because the formula accounts for savings, which is an example of a **leakage**. A leakage is NOT directly used for spending in the short run. An **injection**, such as investment spending, is the opposite of a leakage.

If there is an increase in taxes, multiply the negative tax multiplier by the change in taxes to see the potential decrease in real GDP. If there is a decrease in taxes, do the same thing, but ignore the negative sign to see the potential increase in real GDP.

Lastly, let's consider something known as the **balanced budget multiplier of fiscal policy.** If the government increases spending (an expansionary fiscal policy) and increases income taxes (a contractionary fiscal policy) by the same amount of money, the multiplier is equal to 1. Real GDP will still increase because spending is more powerful than taxes.

Bonus: What causes the short-run aggregate supply curve to shift?

The short-run aggregate supply (SRAS) curve can also shift in the short run. Anything that causes resource costs to change will cause a shift in SRAS.

Changes in resource prices, inflation expectations, productivity, and tax incentives to suppliers are the most common determinants of the short-run aggregate supply curve.

A **negative supply shock**, or sudden increase in the price of a resource, will cause a leftward shift of SRAS. This causes a higher equilibrium price level and higher unemployment (stagflation).

NB4. Banking & Monetary Policy (Macro)

#1. What is money?

Money should contain several qualities for it to be efficient for an economy. For example, money should be accepted, convenient, portable, and divisible. Here is a list of the three key functions of money:

1. **Medium of exchange** (it buys you things)
2. **Stores value** (it holds its worth over time)
3. **Standard of value** (it's a measuring tool of wealth)

Modern economies use **fiat money**, which means that the money has no intrinsic value. In other words, it is money because the government says so. Fiat money is not backed by gold or silver; it is backed by our faith in the government and monetary system.

#2. How do we define the money supply?

The **money supply** (money stock) is monitored and controlled by the central bank, known as the Federal Reserve in the U.S. There are three basic definitions of the money supply:

1. **M1** consists of currency, coin, **checkable (demand) deposits**, and traveler's checks
2. **M2** consists of M1 plus savings deposits and small time deposits (or savings instruments less than $100,000
3. **M3** consists of M2 plus large time deposits (greater than $100,000) and institutional money market accounts

#3. How does a bank's balance sheet work?

A bank's **balance sheet**, or t-account, lists the **assets** (what it owns) and **liabilities** (what it owes) of the institution. The two sides of the balance sheet must equal each other after a transaction is made.

Balance Sheet: Commercial Bank

Assets		Liabilities
Required Reserves $3,000		Demand Deposits $20,000
Excess Reserves	$5,000	
Loans	$12,000	

In this balance sheet, $20,000 was deposited into checking accounts. These demand deposits are liabilities since the bank must pay depositors this money on demand.

The bank stores the deposits in reserve accounts, which are recorded as assets. Banks must keep a percentage of the demand deposits as required reserves. The central bank sets the **reserve requirement**. In this balance sheet, the reserve requirement is 15% because $3,000 is 15% of $20,000.

This bank can hold the other $17,000 as **excess reserves**, which is important because a bank creates money when it lends from excess reserves. This bank already lent out $12,000. Presently, it can legally lend an additional $5,000 from excess reserves.

If a bank cannot meet its reserve requirement, it can borrow from another bank at the **federal funds interest rate,** or from the Federal Reserve at the **discount rate**.

#4. What is the relationship between interest rates and spending?

There is an **inverse relationship between interest rates and private spending**. When interest rates are low, businesses and households have more incentive to borrow from banks. More borrowing leads to more investment spending and consumer spending.

These ideas are also reflected in the **money market** by the **money demand curve**. As the nominal interest rate falls, there is a greater quantity of money demanded by the private sector. When the interest rate is low, the opportunity cost of holding money is low. Please note

that the **money supply curve** is vertical because it is set
by the central bank.

Money Market: Equilibrium Interest Rate

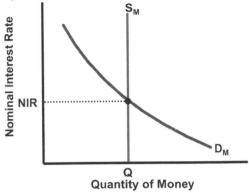

As interest rates increase, businesses and households
have less incentive to borrow from banks. Less
borrowing leads to less investment spending and
consumer spending. When interest rates are high, the
opportunity cost of holding money is high. There is
more incentive to save, rather than to spend.

#5. What is monetary policy?

The Federal Reserve is the central bank of the U.S. It
has several tools of monetary policy that influences
money supply and interest rates. Here are the major
monetary policy tools:

1. **Open Market Operations**: When the Fed buys
   or sells government bonds/securities to
   change the money supply and interest rates, the
   Fed targets the federal funds rate (bank-to-bank
   interest rate for short-term loans) through
   open market operations. If the Fed wants to
   increase money supply and reduce interest
   rates, then it buys bonds. If the Fed wants to reduce
   the money supply and increase interest rates, then it
   sells bonds.

2. **Discount Rate**: The Fed can increase or decrease the interest rate it charges banks for short-term loans. When the Fed lowers the discount rate, the money supply increases. When it raises the discount rate, the money supply decreases.
3. **Reserve Requirement**: The Fed can reduce the reserve ratio, which means banks can lend more of its excess reserves to increase the money supply. It can also raise the reserve ratio, which reduces a bank's excess reserves and the money supply.

#6. How does an expansionary monetary policy work in the short run?

An **expansionary ("easy") monetary policy** makes most sense during a recession. The Fed will **buy bonds on the open market**. It can also decrease the discount rate or decrease the reserve ratio.

In the **money market**, this is represented by a rightward shift of the vertical money supply curve. This will **reduce nominal interest rates** and cause an increase in investment spending and consumer spending.

Money Market: Money Supply Shifts Right

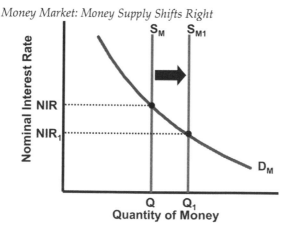

As a result of the increases in investment and consumption, aggregate demand will shift to the right,

Real GDP will increase, price level will increase, and unemployment will decrease.

AD/AS: Rightward Shift of Aggregate Demand

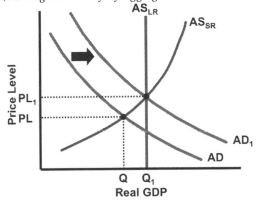

#7. How does a contractionary monetary policy work in the short run?

A **contractionary ("tight") monetary policy** makes most sense during periods of high inflation. The Fed will **sell bonds on the open market**. It can also increase the discount rate or increase the reserve ratio.

In the **money market**, this is represented by a leftward shift of the vertical money supply curve. This will raise interest rates, and decrease investment and consumer spending.

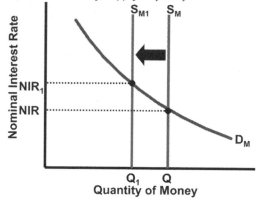

As a result of the decrease in investment and consumer spending, aggregate demand will shift to the left, real GDP will decrease, price level will decrease, and unemployment will increase.

AD/AS: Leftward Shift of Aggregate Demand

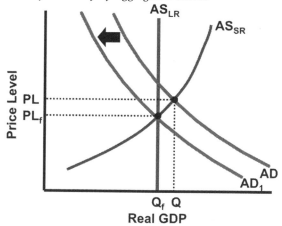

#8. What is the relationship between interest rates and bond prices?

Interest rates and bond prices have an **inverse relationship**. When interest rates are low, money is cheap and the opportunity cost of holding money is low; people can afford to put their money into bonds. An increase in demand for bonds leads to higher bond prices.

As interest rates rise, money is expensive and people cannot afford to hold on to as many bonds. This pushes bond prices down.

#9. What is the money multiplier?

When money is deposited into a bank, excess reserves rise, which increases the lending capability of the bank and the entire banking system. This is because new loans create new checkable deposits, which then create new loans in another bank and then new checkable deposits, and so on.

The **money multiplier**, also known as the deposit expansion multiplier, is calculated using the reserve ratio set by the central bank.

$$\text{Money Multiplier} = \frac{1}{\text{Reserve Ratio}}$$

As the reserve ratio falls, the money creating potential of the banking system increases. As the reserve ratio rises, the money creating potential of the banking system decreases.

#10. How do you use the money multiplier?

Here are formulas to estimate how much the money supply can potentially increase when banks lend out all excess reserves. The first two formulas are based on an initial demand deposit into a bank:

*Change in money supply from a demand deposit = Excess Reserves of initial deposit X Multiplier

*Change in demand deposits in banking system = Initial deposit X Multiplier

The next two formulas are useful for monetary policy:

*Change in money supply by open market operation =
  Bond purchase or sale by the Fed X Multiplier

*Change in new loans by open market operation =
  Excess reserves of initial bond purchase X Multiplier

Bonus: How do you determine the present value and future value of money?

Let's assume that you receive $10 today (the present) and the interest rate on your savings account is 5%, and you want to determine the value of that $10 in one year (the future). You would use the following formula to determine the future value of money:

Future Value = Present Value (1 + Interest Rate)^{Years}

In one year that $10 will be worth $10.50
$$\$10.50 = \$10 \, (1 + 0.05)^1$$

Now let's assume that you will receive $10 in one year and want to determine the present value of that $10 you will receive in the future. Here is the equation for the present value of money:

Present Value = Future Value / (1 + Interest Rate)^{Years}

The present value of that $10 in the future is $9.52
$$\$9.52 = \$10 \, / \, (1 + 0.05)^1$$

The **time value of money** formulas used above show that you are better off receiving a dollar today than in the future because the dollar today can earn interest. Interest represents the opportunity cost of holding money—so don't keep all of your hard-earned cash in the sock drawer!

NB5. Policies & Growth (Macro)

#1. How do the ideas of classical economists and Keynesian economists differ?

There are several references to classical and Keynesian economic theories in previous chapters. While there are many differences between the two schools of thought, here are five simple things to remember about each:

Classical economic theory
1. Focus on the economy over the **long run**
2. Economy will **self-correct** because markets are efficient
3. More savings leads to more investment
4. Wages and prices are flexible
5. No need for active government involvement

Keynesian economic theory
1. Focus on the economy in the **short run**
2. Economy will NOT always self-correct
3. More savings leads to less consumption
4. Wages and prices are "sticky" going down
5. **Active fiscal and monetary policies are necessary**

#2. What are some economic theories that are critical of government policy?

There are many economic critics of fiscal and monetary policy actions. Here are some of those ideas:

Monetarism argues that the central bank often mismanages the money supply and causes unnecessary inflation. When the Fed increases the money supply, it cannot increase real GDP and alleviate unemployment. It will only increase nominal GDP and therefore inflation. This argument can be seen in the monetary **equation of exchange:**

$$MV = PQ$$

"M" is money stock, "V" is velocity (how often $1 is spent in a year), "P" is price level, and "Q" is real GDP. Multiplying P and Q gives us nominal GDP. Velocity is relatively stable so an increase in the money supply will cause inflation, and not guarantee an increase in real GDP.

Monetarists propose **monetary rule** for policy makers, which states that the Fed should only increase the money supply by an amount that is equal to the expected growth rate of the economy.

The ideas of **neutrality of money** and **quantity theory of money** are similar in that the Fed cannot alter real GDP.

Rational expectation theory also dislikes active economic policies by the government and central bank. Rational expectation theory argues that people adjust their economic decisions based on the anticipated outcomes of policies. For example, if the Fed announces it will buy bonds and keep interest rates low, people raise their inflation expectations and ask for higher wages. This reduces output as the Fed is trying to increase output.

Supply-side economic theory focuses on shifting aggregate supply instead of aggregate demand. In theory, this is a good way to deal with **stagflation** (high inflation and unemployment caused by a leftward shift of short-run aggregate supply). For example, if there is a negative supply shock, the government can reduce taxes for all producers. This would lower the costs of production and shift short-run aggregate supply to the right. Inflation and unemployment would fall.

#3. How do you illustrate long-run economic growth?

Long-run economic growth occurs when there is an increase in real GDP or real GDP per capita over time. The main **causes of long-run economic growth** are:

1. Increased quantity of resources
2. Improved quality of resources
3. Improved education and training programs
4. Increased productivity and new technology

You can illustrate long run economic growth in two ways:
1. Rightward shift of the **production possibilities curve**

PPC: Outward Shift

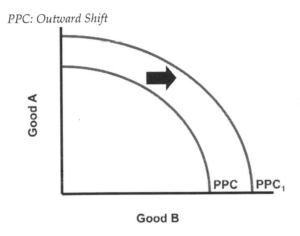

2. Rightward shift of the **long-run aggregate supply curve**

AD/AS: Rightward Shift of Long-Run Aggregate Supply

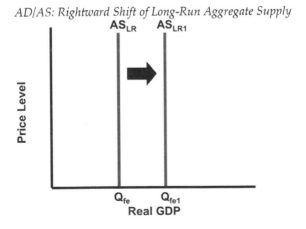

#4. What is the relationship between real interest rates and long-run economic growth?

There is an **inverse relationship between real interest rates and long-run economic growth**. When real interests rise, investment spending falls. Businesses have less incentive to invest in research and development projects, which could lead to technological breakthroughs in production. Businesses are also less likely to replace depreciated capital goods. The growth of **capital stock** (all of a nation's capital goods) will decrease and the long-run growth rate will fall.

When real interest rates are low, businesses are more likely to increase investment spending and develop new technology. This will increase the formation of capital stock and the growth rate of the economy.

#5. What is the crowding out effect of expansionary fiscal policy?

The **crowding out effect** is an unintended consequence of expansionary fiscal policy. When the government increases spending, it borrows from the **loanable funds market**. The government finances the increased spending by issuing new bonds. This causes **real interest rates to rise**. The increase in interest rates causes households and businesses to cut back on spending. This means that consumption and gross investment are "crowded out" by the expansionary fiscal policy that caused real interest rates to rise.

The loanable funds market illustrates the equilibrium real interest rate resulting from the supply (lenders) and demand (borrowers) of loanable funds. **When the government borrows, the demand for loanable funds will increase.**

Loanable Funds Market: Demand Shifts Right

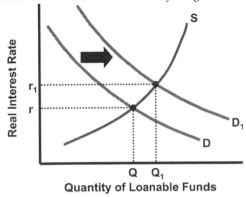

Another interpretation is that the government reduces the private sector's supply of loanable funds. Both situations show that when the government spends more to increase aggregate demand, the real interest will rise.

Loanable Funds Market: Private Supply Shifts Left

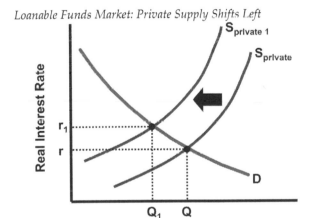

Remember, when the government increases spending, aggregate demand will increase. However, the increase in aggregate demand may not reach its true potential because of the increased interest rate caused by the government's borrowing (greater budget deficit). **This can be detrimental to long-run economic growth.**

#6. How does a change in savings affect the loanable funds market?

The loanable funds market shows the relationship between the real interest rate and quantity of loanable funds.

If there is an **increase in savings** by the private sector, the supply of loanable funds increases (shifts right) causing the real interest rate to fall. When the real interest rate decreases, investment spending will increase. This is good for the growth of capital stock and long-run economic growth.

Loanable Funds Market: Supply Shifts Right

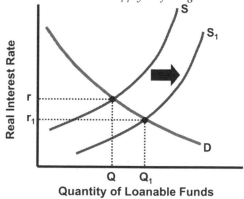

In NB6, you will see that low real interest rates depreciate the value of currency because foreigners will get a lower return on bonds. When the currency depreciates, net exports increase as the goods look cheaper to foreigners.

If there is a **decrease in savings** by the private sector, the supply of loanable funds decreases (shifts left) causing the real interest rate to rise. When the real interest rate increases, investment spending will decrease. This is bad for the growth of capital stock and slows down the rate of long-run economic growth.

40

In NB6, you will see that high real interest rates appreciate the value of currency because foreigners are attracted to the higher returns on bonds. When a currency appreciates, net exports decrease as goods look expensive to foreigners.

#7. How does a change in aggregate demand relate to the short-run Phillips curve?

The **short-run Phillips curve** is a model that shows the inverse relationship between inflation and unemployment. The unemployment rate is measured on the x-axis and the inflation rate is measured on the y-axis.

When aggregate demand shifts to the right, price level increases (inflation rises) and real GDP increases (unemployment falls). Therefore, **point-to-point movement leftward along the short-run Phillips curve represents an increase in aggregate demand.**

Short-Run Phillips Curve: Point-to-Point Movement

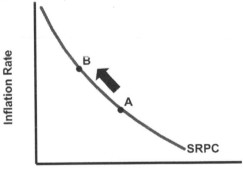

When aggregate demand shifts to the left, price level decreases (inflation falls) and real GDP decreases (unemployment rises). Therefore, **point-to-point movement rightward along the short-run Phillips curve represents a decrease in aggregate demand.**

41

#8. How does a change in short-run aggregate supply relate to the short-run Phillips curve?

When there is a shift of the short-run aggregate supply curve, the short-run Phillips curve will also shift. If there is a rightward shift of the short-run aggregate supply curve, the short-run Phillips curve will shift left. This is because inflation and unemployment both decrease.

Short-Run Phillips Curve: Leftward Shift

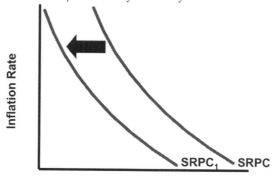

Unemployment Rate

If there is a leftward shift of the short-run aggregate supply curve, the short-run Phillips curve will shift right. This is because inflation and unemployment increase at the same time (stagflation).

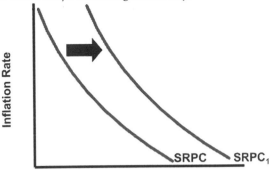

Short-Run Phillips Curve: Rightward Shift

#9. How do inflation expectations affect the short-run Phillips curve?

Inflation expectations wield a lot of power within an economy. In NB3, we saw that changes in inflation expectations shift the short-run aggregate supply curve. **When inflation expectations rise, resource costs rise and short-run aggregate supply shifts left causing high prices and high unemployment.** This is represented by a rightward shift of the short-run Phillips curve.

Here are two important ideas to remember about the AD/AS model and the Phillips curve:
1. When aggregate demand shifts one way, move point-to-point the opposite way along the short-run Phillips curve.
2. When short-run aggregate supply shifts one way, the short-run Phillips curve shifts the opposite way.

#10. What is the relationship between inflation and unemployment in the long run?

In the long run, there is **no tradeoff between inflation and unemployment.** The economy will always return to full employment, which is represented by the long-run

Phillips curve. It is a vertical line at the economy's natural rate of unemployment.

Phillips Curve: Long Run & Short Run

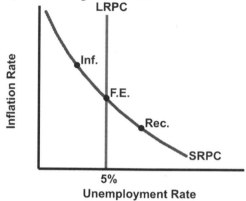

If the economy is operating to the right of the long-run Phillips curve in the short run, the economy is experiencing a recessionary gap (high unemployment). If the economy is operating to the left of the long-run Phillips curve, there is an inflationary gap (high inflation).

NB6. International Sector (Macro)

#1. What is the difference between a current account transaction and a capital account transaction?

The **balance of payments** system keeps record of all foreign transactions. There are two main accounts in the balance of payments system, the current account and capital account. The **current account** consists of imports, exports, and foreign transfer payments. The **capital account** (or financial account) consists of real assets and financial assets. A real asset is property or a factory. A financial asset is a stock or bond.

When foreign money flows into our current account as a result of an export, our current account is **credited**. When our currency leaves the capital account after purchasing a foreign apartment complex, the capital account is **debited**.

If one account shows a surplus, the other will show a deficit. In the end, the two accounts should balance.

#2. How does a trade deficit affect a nation's economy in the short run?

A **trade deficit** occurs when a nation's imports are greater than its exports. Net exports are negative and the current account is showing a deficit. When a trade deficit increases in the short run, aggregate demand shifts to the left. The price level decreases, real GDP falls, and unemployment rises.

If a nation's exports are greater than its imports, it has a **trade surplus** or current account surplus. When net exports increase, aggregate demand will increase.

In the long run, exports and imports will balance out.

#3. How do you determine whether a country will benefit from trade?

To determine whether two countries should specialize and trade, use the law of comparative advantage (Ricardian model). In NB1, we said that you simply look at the opportunity costs of production. The country with the lowest relative opportunity cost will specialize in the production of that good and export that good if trade occurs.

To determine if trade terms are beneficial, simply divide the imports by the exports for each country.

If the imports divided by the exports are greater than the opportunity cost of the good that the country is exporting, then it is a good trade for the country.

If it works out for both countries then the trade will occur as both will benefit.

#4. What are some barriers to international trade?

In the long run, the gains from international trade are greater than the losses. In the short run, trade can hurt domestic producers and cause domestic unemployment, which can lead to the implementation of trade barriers by policy makers.

One type of trade barrier is a **tariff**; a protectionist tool that taxes imports. This raises the costs of foreign goods to keep domestic industries alive. However, higher prices hurt consumers.

This market graph below shows the effects of a per-unit tariff. DP represents the domestic price, WP represents the world price, and $WP+T$ represents the world price with the tariff.

Supply & Demand: Effects of a Per-Unit Tariff

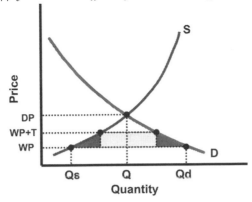

The lightly shaded rectangle is the total tariff revenue collected by the government, and the two shaded triangles represent the deadweight loss (inefficiency) created by the tariff. We will revisit this graph in NB11.

Other tools of protectionist policy include **import quotas** (legal limits), complicated licensing procedures, and high quality standards.

A more unfortunate barrier to trade is a global military conflict that cuts off supply lines between trade partners; or perhaps, a war between two trading partners.

#5. What factors will cause a currency to appreciate in value?

The international value of currency will appreciate (increase in value) relative to another currency due to the following factors:

1. **Interest rates increase** – Foreigners will demand more bonds when interest rates rise because foreigners will receive greater returns. There will be more demand for currency so the currency will appreciate.

2. **Tastes and preferences for goods increase** – If foreigners demand products produced over here, then there will be more demand for

currency and the currency will appreciate.

3. **Inflation decreases** – If prices are relatively lower here than overseas, then foreigners will demand goods over here. There will be more demand for currency so the currency will appreciate.

4. **Income decreases** – If this economy becomes weaker than a foreign economy, this economy cannot afford to buy as many foreign goods. This economy will supply fewer units of currency to the foreign exchange market so the currency will appreciate.

5. **Foreign direct investment inflows** – If foreigners want to build factories over here, then they must first acquire our currency to do so. This increased demand for our currency will lead to its appreciation.

#6. What factors will cause currency to depreciate in value?

The international value of currency will depreciate (decrease in value relative to another currency) due to the following factors:

1. **Interest rates decrease** – Foreigners will demand fewer bonds when interest rates fall because foreigners will receive less return on interest-bearing assets.

2. **Tastes and preferences for goods decrease** – If foreigners demand fewer products produced over here, then the currency will depreciate.

3. **Inflation increases** – If prices are relatively higher over here than overseas, then foreigners will not want our goods and we will want to import cheaper goods from overseas.

4. **Incomes increase** – If this economy becomes stronger than a foreign economy, the foreign economy cannot afford as many of our goods. However, we can afford to purchase more foreign

goods.

5. **Foreign direct investment outflows** – If we want to build more factories overseas than foreigners want to build here, our currency will depreciate. We would increase the supply of our currency as we demand more foreign currency.

#7. How do exchange rates work?

An **exchange rate** is determined by supply and demand in the foreign exchange market. It is how much of one country's currency it takes to buy one unit of another country's currency.

For example, it might cost 0.73 euro to buy $1 US this month. If it is costs 0.5 euro to buy $1 US next month, the euro has appreciated in value because it takes fewer euros to buy $1 US. This means that the dollar has depreciated against the euro.

With the exchange rates from the example above, $1.37 US will buy 1 euro this month. Next month, it costs $2 US to buy 1 euro. Again, the euro appreciated and the US dollar depreciated. Exchange rates and the value of a currency are all relative.

#8. How do you illustrate the foreign exchange market?

To graph a foreign exchange market, you need two different currencies to compare. For example, the market for US dollars needs to show how much of a foreign currency is needed to buy $1 US.

In the market for US dollars, the *Quantity of US Dollars* goes on the x-axis. On the y-axis, you put the foreign currency price of the US dollar. This graph shows the **market for US dollars** and the euro price of a dollar.

Foreign Exchange Market: US Dollar

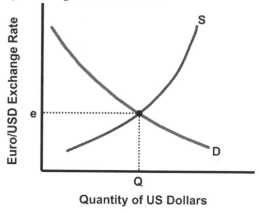

If the euro price of a US dollar increases, it takes more euros to buy one US dollar. This means that the US dollar appreciated and the euro depreciated.

The next graph shows the **market for euros** and the US dollar price of a euro.

Foreign Exchange Market: Euro

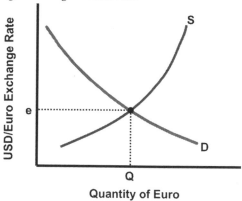

If the US dollar price of a euro increases, it takes more dollars to buy a euro. This means that the euro appreciated and the US dollar depreciated.

#9. How do you show the effects of increased interest rates using the foreign exchange market?

Interest rates are an important determinant of a country's currency value. If a central bank pursues a "tight" monetary policy that causes interest rates to rise (or an expansionary fiscal policy that causes interest rates to rise), then there would be **more foreign demand for the country's interest-bearing assets (bonds)**. This will lead to an increase in demand for the currency and appreciate its value.

Foreign Exchange Market: Demand Shifts Right

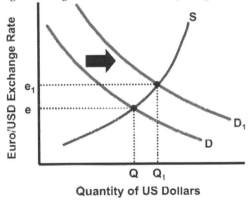

When a country's currency appreciates, its goods look more expensive to foreigners, while foreign goods look cheap. This will reduce the country's net exports and shift aggregate demand to the left.

Remember, high interest rates also harm long-run economic growth as it slows down the growth of capital stock.

#10. How do you show the effects of a decrease in aggregate income using the foreign exchange market?

Suppose one economy is in recession while another country's economy is strong. The country in recession won't be able to import as many goods since income is low. Therefore, it will **supply less currency to the foreign exchange market**. When this happens, the value of currency will appreciate. This diagram assumes that the U.S. is in recession and the German economy is doing well.

Foreign Exchange Market: Supply Shifts Left

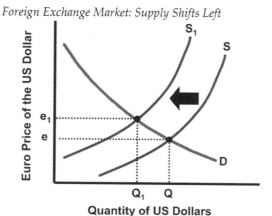

Bonus: Why are interest rates important?

As you know, interest rates play several vital roles within an economy. However, it can be difficult for students to grasp them all. Here is a chart that summarizes the main effects of interest rate changes:

Interest Rates Increase	Interest Rates Decrease
Consumption & investment spending decrease	Consumption & investment spending increase
Aggregate demand decreases	Aggregate demand increases
Bond prices decrease	Bond prices increase
Growth of capital stock slows	Growth of capital stock increases
Long-run economic growth slows	Long-run economic growth increases
International demand for bonds & currency increase	International demand for bonds & currency decrease
Currency appreciates	Currency depreciates
Net exports decrease	Net exports increase

No Bull Review Sheet – Macroeconomics

Top 10 Macroeconomics Concepts to Know
1. Fiscal policy tools – changes in spending & taxes to shift AD in the short run toward full employment, *NB3*
2. Spending (1/MPS) & tax multiplier (-MPC/MPS) – multiply by change in spending (or taxes) to find change in Real GDP, *NB2*
3. Crowding out effect – expansionary fiscal policy raises interest rates and reduces consumption & investment; slows growth rate, *NB5*
4. Monetary policy tools – open market operations (buy bonds inc. MS & sell bonds dec. MS), discount rate (Fed to bank IR), & reserve requirement, *NB4*
5. Money multiplier (1/RR) – multiply by bond purchase for change in money supply, *NB4*
6. Interest rate relationships – IR-spending, IR-growth rate, & IR-bond prices are inverse; IR-currency value is direct, *NB6*
7. Long run economic growth factors - #resources, education, training, tech, productivity, *NB5*
8. Effects of unanticipated inflation – hurts lenders, savers, fixed income earners; helps debtors, fixed payment makers, *NB2*
9. AD/AS & Phillips curve – if AD shifts, point-to-point opposite way on SRPC; if SRAS shifts, SRPC shifts opposite way, *NB5*
10. Determinants of appreciation (high IR, high tastes, low PL, low income) & depreciation of currency (low IR, low tastes, high PL, high income), *NB6*

Top 5 Macroeconomics Models to Master
1. AD/AS Graphs, *NB3*
2. Money Market Graphs, *NB4*
3. Loanable Funds Market Graphs, *NB5*
4. Short-Run and Long-Run Phillips Curves, *NB5*
5. Foreign Exchange Market Graphs, *NB6*

Other important models:
Production Possibilities Graphs, *NB1*; Supply and Demand, *NB1*

Top 5 Macroeconomics Formulas to Master
1. Nominal GDP & Real GDP, *NB2*
2. Fisher Equation (Real Interest Rate), *NB2*
3. Spending Multiplier & Change in Output, *NB3*
4. Money Multiplier & Change in Money Supply, *NB4*
5. Equation of Exchange, *NB5*

Other important formulas:
Unemployment Rate, *NB2*; Inflation Rate, *NB2*

NB7. Utility & Elasticity (Micro)

#1. What is the relationship between total utility and marginal utility?

As consumers increase their purchases of any product, their total utility (satisfaction) from consumption initially increases at an increasing rate. At some point, the total utility will continue to increase with more units purchased, but at a decreasing rate. When the rate of increase slows, consumers are experiencing diminishing marginal utility (refer to NB1). Lastly, as consumers continue to purchase even more quantities, the total utility will reach its peak and then eventually fall.

The marginal utility curve is the slope of the total utility curve ($\Delta TU / \Delta Q$). Initially, marginal utility increases as quantity increases; this is known as increasing marginal utility, which is then followed by diminishing marginal utility. **When marginal utility becomes 0, total utility is maximized.** When marginal utility becomes negative, total utility falls.

#2. How do you calculate the utility-maximizing combination of goods for consumers?

When a buyer purchases two types of goods, we can determine the utility-maximizing quantities of each good using the following equation:

$$\frac{\text{Marginal Utility of X}}{\text{Price of X}} = \frac{\text{Marginal Utility of Y}}{\text{Price of Y}}$$

The ratios must equal one another. If you need the marginal utility/price to decrease, then buy more units of that good. This is because of the law of diminishing marginal utility (as you buy additional units, marginal utility decreases).

If you need the marginal utility/price to increase, then buy less of the good.

#3. How do you identify the area of consumer and producer surplus in a market?

When a market is in equilibrium, the sum of consumer and producer surplus is maximized. A **consumer surplus** exists when the market price that a consumer pays for a product is less than what he or she is willing to pay. Suppose you are willing to pay $15 for a movie ticket and the market price is $10. You have a consumer surplus of $5. In a supply and demand graph, the area of consumer surplus is above the equilibrium price and under the demand curve.

A **producer surplus** exists when the market price is greater than what the producer is willing to sell for. This is the area under the equilibrium price and above the supply curve.

Supply & Demand: Consumer & Producer Surplus

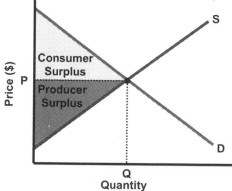

#4. What are the determinants of the price elasticity of demand?

In economics, elasticity translates to responsiveness. The price elasticity of demand measures how responsive consumers are to changes in the price of a good. The formula is:

$$\frac{\text{Percent Change in Quantity Demand}}{\text{Percent Change in Price}}$$

When calculating price elasticity of demand, ignore the negative sign. Demand will be price elastic when elasticity is greater than 1. **Goods with many substitutes and/or goods that take up a large percentage of one's income tend to be elastic**. This means that consumers are sensitive to price changes.

Demand is price inelastic when elasticity is less than 1. **Inelastic goods are necessities and/or goods that take up a small percentage of one's income.** This means that consumers are NOT sensitive to price changes.

#5. How is the slope of a demand curve related to the price elasticity of demand?

The slope of a good's demand curve is NOT the same as the price elasticity of demand. For example, slope can be constant while the elasticity can change along the curve. **At low prices along a demand curve, demand can be inelastic, and at high prices demand can be elastic.**

However, if a good has a steep demand curve, the good's demand is more inelastic than a good with a flat demand curve.

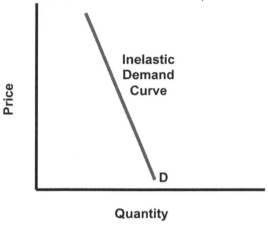

If a good has a flatter demand curve, the good's demand is relatively price elastic.

Elastic Demand Curve: High Consumer Responsiveness

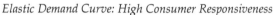

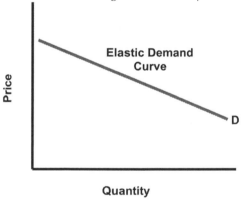

#6. What does a vertical and horizontal demand curve indicate about consumer responsiveness?

There are two extreme cases of price elasticity of demand: perfectly inelastic ($E_d=0$) and perfectly elastic $E_d=\infty$) demand.

A **perfectly inelastic demand curve is a vertical line**. This means that there will be no change in quantity demanded when the prices changes. Consumers are completely unresponsive. This can occur if a good is an absolute necessity and has zero substitutes.

Perfectly Inelastic Demand Curve: No Consumer Responsiveness

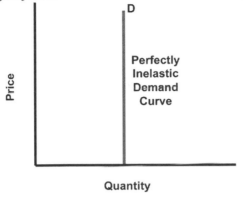

A **horizontal line represents a perfectly elastic demand curve**. This means that the slightest increase in price will lead to zero quantities demanded. Consumers are completely responsive. This can occur when there are many perfect substitutes. For example, a perfectly competitive firm has a perfectly elastic demand curve (see NB9).

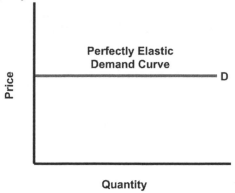

#7. How is total revenue related to the price elasticity of demand?

The **total revenue test** is a great way to estimate whether a good's demand is price elastic or inelastic. You need to see how the price changes relative to the total revenue (Price x Quantity).

If price and total revenue move in opposite directions, consumers are responsive to changes in price so demand is price elastic ($E_d>1$).

If price and total revenue move in the same direction, consumers are NOT very responsive to the change in price so demand is price inelastic ($E_d<1$).

If total revenue is constant when the price changes, then demand is unit elastic ($E_d=1$).

#8. How do you determine income elasticity of demand?

The income elasticity of demand measures how responsive consumers are to changes in income. The formula is:

$$\frac{\textbf{Percent Change in Quantity Demand}}{\textbf{Percent Change in Income}}$$

If income elasticity is positive, then the good is a normal good. Luxury goods are greater than 1 and necessities are less than 1. If income elasticity is negative, then the good is an inferior good.

#9. How do you determine the cross-price elasticity of demand?

The cross-price elasticity of demand is useful in determining whether two goods are related to one another. The formula is:

Percent Change in Quantity Demand of Good X
Percent Change in Price of Good Y

If the cross-price elasticity between the goods is positive, then the goods are substitutes. If the cross-price elasticity is negative, then the goods are complements. If the goods are unrelated, then the number should be close to zero.

#10. How do you determine the price elasticity of supply?

The price elasticity of supply measures how responsive sellers are to changes in price. The formula is:

Percent Change in Quantity Supply
Percent Change in Price

If the price elasticity of supply is greater than 1, supply is elastic. This means that sellers are sensitive to changes in price.

When the price elasticity of supply is less than 1, supply is inelastic. This means that sellers are NOT very responsive to changes in price.

An elastic supply curve is relatively flatter than an inelastic supply curve, and an inelastic supply curve is relatively steeper than an elastic supply curve.

The most important determinant of the elasticity of supply is the amount of time that the sellers have to adjust production. A longer period of time (the long run) means supply is more elastic. A shorter period of time (the short run) means supply is more inelastic. Other determinants include the availability of resources and the complexity of the production process.

In NB11, we will see that sellers experience a greater burden of a per-unit tax than buyers, when supply is more inelastic than demand.

NB8. Costs of Production (Micro)

#1. How does the law of diminishing marginal returns work?

As a firm increases its employment of an economic input such as labor, its **total product** (TP) will increase. Initially, total product will rise at an increasing rate; then the total product will continue to rise, but at a decreasing rate. This is due to the law of diminishing marginal returns. Here are the three stages of production for a firm:

1. **Increasing marginal returns**
   When **marginal product** (ΔTP/ΔInputs) increases, total product is rising at an increasing rate.

2. **Diminishing marginal returns**
   When marginal product falls, total product rises at a decreasing rate. This means that when a firm employs additional units of a resource, the additional output added to the total product by the next resource will decline. This occurs when variable resources are added to fixed capital goods.

3. **Negative marginal returns**
   When total product is at its highest level, marginal product is 0. When total product falls, marginal product becomes negative and the firm experiences negative marginal returns.

#2. What is the relationship between the average product curve and marginal product curve?

The marginal product and average product curves initially increase then decrease due to the law of diminishing marginal returns.

Marginal product is the change in total product divided by the change in quantity of resources. **Average product** is the total product divided by the quantity of economic resources.

The average product reaches its peak when it intersects the marginal product curve.

Marginal Product & Average Product Curves

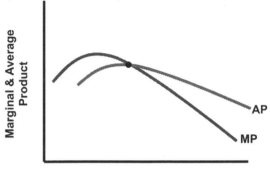

Quantity of Labor

#3. Why are economic profits often less than accounting profits?

An **economic profit** occurs when a firm's total revenue (Price x Quantity) exceeds its total economic costs. From an economic standpoint, costs are explicit (paid out to a resource supplier) and implicit (an opportunity cost NOT paid out to a resource supplier).

An **accounting profit** does NOT take into account implicit costs. Therefore, accounting profits will exceed economic profits when an opportunity cost (foregone alternative) is present.

For example, if a firm is breaking even and earning zero economic profit (also known as a normal profit), accounting profits can be positive.

#4. What types of costs does a typical firm face?

There are three types of costs that all firms face:

1. **Fixed costs** (FC) must be paid to resource suppliers regardless of output. An example is rent paid for factory space. When a firm produces zero units of

output, it still pays fixed costs.
2. **Variable costs** (VC) change with output. An example is an hourly employee.
3. **Total costs** (TC) equal fixed costs plus variable costs.

#5. How do you calculate and graph the per-unit costs of a firm?

Per-unit costs are used to derive the average cost curves of a firm. To get average costs, simply divide the total costs by the quantities produced:

$$\text{Average Fixed Cost} = \frac{FC}{Q} \text{ or } ATC - AVC$$

$$\text{Average Variable Cost} = \frac{VC}{Q} \text{ or } ATC - AFC$$

$$\text{Average Total Cost} = \frac{TC}{Q} \text{ or } AFC + AVC$$

The most important cost is marginal cost because marginal costs help determine a firm's optimal level of output:

$$\textbf{Marginal cost} = \frac{\textbf{Change in TC}}{\textbf{Change in Q}}$$

The marginal cost curve is shaped like a checkmark. Marginal costs initially fall then rise as output increases. This is because of diminishing marginal returns.

Per-Unit Cost Curves

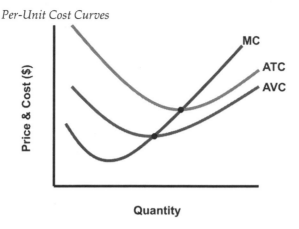

Quantity

The average total cost curve and average variable cost curve are u-shaped. Both curves will reach their lowest points when intersecting the marginal cost curve. The difference between the ATC and AVC represents the average fixed costs. This is why the space between the ATC and AVC curves narrow as output increases.

#6. What is the relationship between total revenue and marginal revenue?

There are three types of revenue to consider for a firm: total revenue, average revenue, and marginal revenue. The revenue formulas are:

Total Revenue = Price x Quantity

Average Revenue = Total Revenue
Quantity

Marginal Revenue = Change in Total Revenue
Change in Output

By calculating a firm's average revenue, we can derive its demand curve. The marginal revenue is the additional revenue a firm gains from producing one more unit of output.

In NB7, we noted the relationship between total revenue and the price elasticity of demand. Now we can link the elasticity of demand to marginal revenue. When marginal revenue is positive, an increase in price will show a decrease in total revenue (demand is elastic). When marginal revenue is negative, an increase in price will show an increase in total revenue (demand is inelastic). **When marginal revenue is 0, total revenue is at its peak.**

Demand Elasticity, Marginal Revenue, & Total Revenue

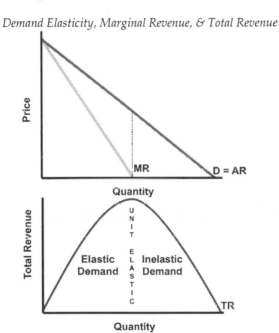

Remember, total revenue and economic profit are NOT the same. A firm prefers to maximize economic profits, NOT total revenue.

#7. How do you determine the level of output where a firm will maximize economic profit?

The profit-maximization rule is that a firm should produce at a level of output where its **marginal revenue equals its marginal cost (MR=MC)**. At this point, a firm will experience its greatest economic profit or minimize its economic losses.

When price is greater than the average total cost at the MR=MC output point, a firm is earning a profit. When price is less than average total cost, a firm takes a loss.

You can also calculate a firm's total revenues and total costs at every output level, and then find the differences to see where profits are maximized.

#8. How will a per-unit tax and lump-sum tax affect a firm's costs and output?

A **per-unit tax discourages production by raising marginal costs** (MC shifts upward). This will decrease the firm's level of output and reduce economic profits. The average total cost and average variable cost curves also shift up, but it's the marginal cost curve that changes the profit-maximizing level of output because the MR=MC point has moved to the left.

A **lump-sum tax does NOT change a firm's level of output** because a lump-sum tax does not change marginal cost. It increases the firm's fixed costs and shifts average total cost upward. This will decrease a firm's economic profit, but not change output.

A **per-unit subsidy encourages more production by lowering marginal costs** (MC shifts down). This will increase the firm's level of output and increase economic profit. The average total cost and average variable cost curves also shift down, but it's the marginal cost curve that changes the profit-maximizing level of output as the MR=MC point has moved to the right.

A **lump-sum subsidy** does NOT change a firm's level of output because a lump-sum subsidy does not change marginal cost. It reduces the firm's fixed costs and shifts the average total cost down. This will increase a firm's economic profit, but not change output.

#9. How does production in the short run compare to the long run?

In the **short run**, a firm can increase its output by employing more variable inputs. The firm can reduce output by hiring fewer variable inputs. It can experience economic profits or economic losses. The firm can also break even or shut down and produce zero units of output. In the short run, the capacity of the plant is fixed.

In the **long run**, a firm can change the quantities of all economic inputs and its plant capacity. Firms can also enter and exit an industry.

#10. What are the three components of the long-run average total cost curve?

The long-run average total cost curve contains three parts: economies of scale, constant returns to scale, and diseconomies of scale.

Economies of scale will occur when long-run average total costs decrease as output increases. This happens because the firm is specializing its productive resources efficiently. Large firms that own many resources and employ advanced technology will experience economies of scale over a larger range of output than smaller firms. The point where the long-run average total cost curve reaches its minimum is known as **minimum efficient scale**.

Constant returns to scale exists when long-run average total costs stay the same as output increases.

Diseconomies of scale will occur when long-run average total costs increase as output increases. This happens as expanding firms experience inefficiencies during the production process.

Long-Run Average Total Cost Curve

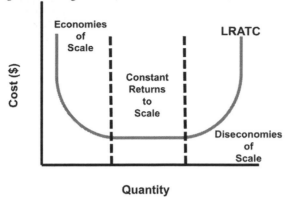

NB9. Product Markets (Micro)

#1. What are the key characteristics of the four market structures?

1. **Perfect Competition**
   -Hundreds of firms selling identical products
   -Market determines price
   -Firm is a "price taker"
   -Very easy for sellers to enter the market
   -Firm experiences **allocative** (price = marginal cost) and **productive efficiency** (price = minimum average total cost) in the long run
   -Firm breaks even in long run
   -Example: Agriculture

2. **Monopolistic Competition**
   -Many firms selling differentiated, but similar products
   -Firm has some control over price
   -Relatively easy for new sellers to enter the market
   -Firm breaks even in long run, but experiences **excess capacity** (average total costs can be lower by increasing output)
   -Example: Clothing

3. **Oligopoly**
   -A few powerful firms selling identical or differentiated products
   -Firm has considerable control over price
   -Difficult for new sellers to enter the market; significant barriers to entry
   -Firm can profit in long run
   -Firms are interdependent
   -Game theory is often used to show a firm's optimal decision and possible payout
   -Example: Video game consoles

4. **Monopoly**
    -One firm selling a unique product
    -Firm is a "price maker"
    -Highly inefficient
    -High barriers to entry
    -High profits in long run
    -Example: Electricity, although the firm is often
     regulated

#2. How do you graph a perfectly competitive firm earning a short-run economic profit?

When graphing perfect competition, it is a good idea to graph the market and firm side-by-side so that the market equilibrium is lined up with the firm's horizontal marginal revenue curve.

Short-Run Economic Profit: The market (industry) graph is a simple supply and demand graph. For the firm, the market price equals the firm's marginal revenue, which is also the firm's perfectly elastic demand curve. In NB8, we said that a firm maximizes its profit where marginal revenue (MR) equals marginal cost (MC). The MR=MC output point must exceed the average total cost curve to show a short-run profit.

Perfectly Competitive Market & Firm: Short-Run Economic Profit

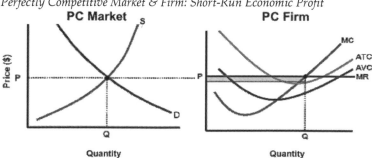

Here is a closer look at the firm with the shaded region representing the area of total economic profit:

Perfectly Competitive Firm Earning Short-Run Economic Profit

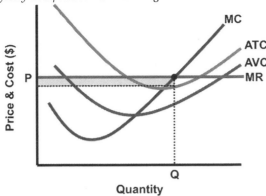

#3. How do you graph a perfectly competitive firm with a short-run economic loss?

A firm will operate at an **economic loss in the short run** as long as it can afford to cover its variable costs. For the firm, the MR=MC output point is below the average total cost curve. The price (MR) exceeds the average variable cost curve. If the firm shuts down, it would still have to pay fixed costs. It loses less money by operating at a loss.

Perfectly Competitive Firm Taking Short-Run Economic Loss

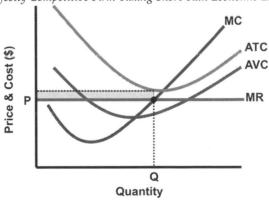

Shutdown Case: If a firm cannot cover its variable costs, it will shut down and produce 0 units of output, but still pay its fixed cost. This means that the price is less than the minimum point of the AVC curve. **Because firms will only produce above the minimum AVC point, the marginal cost curve above this point represents the firm's short-run supply curve.**

Perfectly Competitive Firm: Short-Run Shutdown Case

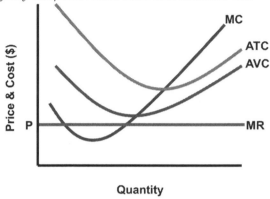

#4. How do you graph a perfectly competitive firm in long-run equilibrium?

In the long run, a perfectly competitive firm will always break even. This occurs where the **MR=MC output point equals the minimum ATC curve.** The firm experiences allocative efficiency (P=MC) and productive efficiency (P=Min. ATC) at the same time. Other terms for the break-even point are normal profit, zero economic profit, and long-run equilibrium.

74

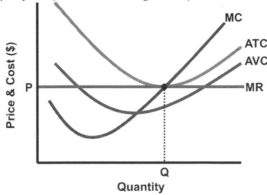

Perfectly Competitive Firm: Long-Run Equilibrium

If a firm is earning a short-run economic profit, more firms will enter the market in the long run. This is because new sellers are hoping to experience profits of their own. However, the market supply curve will shift right causing the price (MR) to decrease. The new MR will equal the firm's minimum ATC and the firm will break even.

If a firm is taking a short-run economic loss, firms will exit the market in the long run. The market supply will shift left and the price (MR) will increase. This results in long-run equilibrium.

#5. How do you graph an unregulated monopoly?

To illustrate an unregulated monopoly with an **economic profit**, the demand curve must exceed the average total cost curve at the MR=MC level of output. Demand is downward sloping for the monopolist since it represents the entire industry's demand. The marginal revenue curve is also downward sloping, but sits below the demand curve. The monopolist will produce in the elastic region of its demand curve. In this region, marginal revenue is greater than 0.

75

Monopoly: Economic Profit

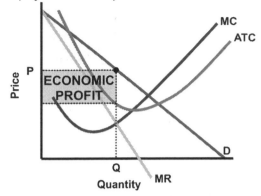

The graph above shows the area of economic profit. The next graph shows the area of **total revenue** at the profit-maximizing level of output:

Monopoly: Area of Total Revenue

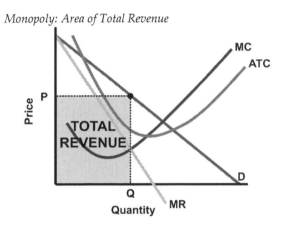

The next graph shows the area of **total economic costs**:

Monopoly: Area of Economic Costs

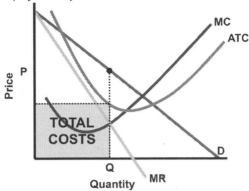

To graph a monopoly taking an **economic loss**, the price must be less than the average total cost curve at the MR=MC level of output. In this example, total costs exceed the firm's total revenue.

Monopoly: Economic Loss

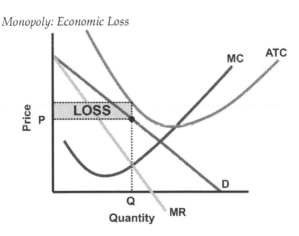

#6. Why are monopolies inefficient compared to competitive market structures?

A profit-maximizing monopolist is inefficient compared to a perfectly competitive market because the monopolist charges a higher price and produces less output. The term for inefficiency in economics is

deadweight loss (shaded below). Since the monopolist charges a price greater than its marginal cost, there is **no allocative efficiency**. Society loses the area between the perfectly competitive output level (D=MC) and the monopolist's output. Also, the monopolist does NOT experience productive efficiency because the ATC curve is NOT at its minimum point at the profit-maximizing level of output.

Monopoly: Area of Deadweight Loss

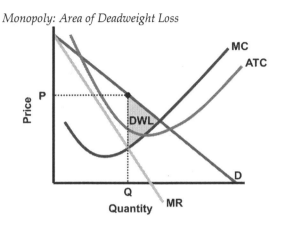

Because of the higher monopoly price, the area of consumer surplus is less than a perfectly competitive market's consumer surplus. Part of the original consumer surplus under a perfectly competitive market will be transferred to the producer. The rest becomes part of the deadweight loss. In the next graph, you can compare the monopoly price and output to the perfectly competitive price and output. The perfectly competitive consumer surplus is the area under the demand curve and above P_{PC}. The consumer surplus under a monopoly is the shaded triangle.

Monopoly: Area of Consumer Surplus

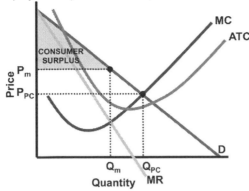

#7. What else should I know about graphing monopolies?

Socially Optimal Regulation: If a monopolist were regulated to produce at the socially optimal level of output, it would produce where the price (demand) intersects the marginal cost curve (P=MC). At this level of output, allocative efficiency is achieved and there is no deadweight loss. This point will maximize the sum of consumer and producer surplus. The graph below shows the socially optimal price (P_{SO}) and quantity (Q_{SO}).

Monopoly: Socially Optimal Price

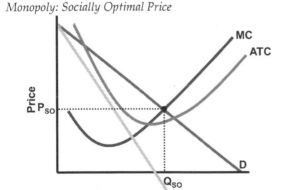

Fair-Return Regulation: If a monopoly is regulated to break even (zero economic profit, normal profit), it will produce at a level of output where price equals average total cost (P=D=ATC). This is known as the fair-return price. Even though there are no economic profits, **accounting profits can still be positive** when there is an opportunity cost. The next graph shows the fair-return price (P_{FR}) and quantity (Q_{FR}).

Monopoly: Fair-Return Price

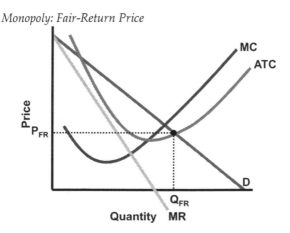

Total Revenue Maximization: The monopolist will maximize total revenue at a level of output where **marginal revenue equals 0** (Q_{TR}). The price is above that point on the demand curve (P_{TR}) and the price elasticity of demand equals 1 (unit elastic).

Monopoly: Total Revenue Maximization

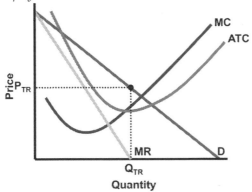

Price Discrimination: If a monopolist practiced perfect price discrimination, profits would increase drastically as the area of consumer surplus would be eliminated. Each consumer would pay the highest price that he or she is willing to pay. The former consumer surplus becomes part of the economic profit, but society will get a more socially efficient level of output (MC=D).

Monopoly: Perfect Price Discrimination

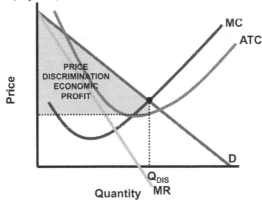

#8. How do you graph a monopolistically competitive firm in the short run?

The cost curves of a monopolistically competitive firm look similar to a monopolist's curves. But by definition, monopolistic competition (many firms) is very different from a monopoly (one firm).

To graph a monopolistically competitive firm earning a **short-run economic profit**, the price must exceed the average total cost curve at the MR=MC level of output. The demand curve should be relatively flatter (more elastic) than a monopolist's demand curve because more substitutes are available to consumers. Here is the profit-maximizing price (P_{MC}) and quantity (Q_{MC}):

Monopolistic Competition: Short-Run Economic Profit

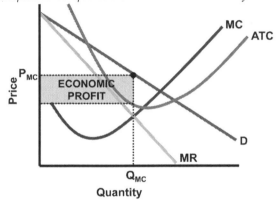

To graph a monopolistically competitive firm taking a **short-run economic loss**, the price must be less than the average total cost curve at the MR=MC level of output. Price should also exceed the average variable cost curve for the firm to produce. Here is the loss-minimizing price (P_{MC}) and quantity (Q_{MC}):

Monopolistic Competition: Short-Run Economic Loss

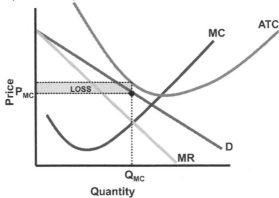

#9. How do you graph a monopolistically competitive firm in long run equilibrium?

In the long run, a monopolistically competitive firm will break even and experience **excess capacity**. The price will equal average total cost at the MR=MC level of output. There is excess capacity because the firm can produce more units at a lower average total cost. Remember, the minimum ATC is on the marginal cost curve to the right of the MR=MC point.

Monopolistic Competition: Long-Run Equilibrium

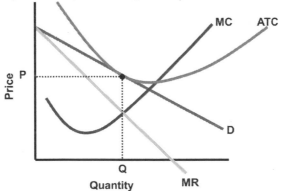

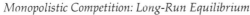

83

This is still inefficient compared to a perfectly competitive market because the price is greater than MC and the price is NOT equal to minimum ATC.

#10. How do you determine a firm's dominant strategy in the oligopoly model?

Game theory is an important topic that comes up in the discussion of oligopoly (more specifically for this course, duopoly) behavior. One of your goals is to determine a firm's **dominant strategy**, or best strategy regardless of an opposing firm's strategy. This will help you find the **Nash equilibrium**.

When reading a game theory matrix, the firm on the left has its payouts on the left in each cell. The firm on the top typically has its payouts on the right in each cell.

In the diagram below, Totally Inc.'s dominant strategy is Strategy A because $2,305 > $2,272 and $2,350 > $2,325. Awesome LLC.'s dominant strategy is also Strategy A because $2,305 > $2,272 and $2,350 > $2,325.

Game Theory Matrix

		Awesome LLC.	
		Strategy A	Strategy B
Totally Inc.	**Strategy A**	$2,305, $2,305	$2,350, $2,272
	Strategy B	$2,272, $2,350	$2,325, $2,325

Therefore, the Nash equilibrium is the cell where both firms play Strategy A. We know that each firm will earn $2,305 when they play their dominant strategies. As long as one firm has a dominant strategy, you can find the Nash equilibrium.

A **prisoner's dilemma** occurs when each firm's respective payouts are greater if each firm does NOT play its dominant strategy. In the game theory matrix above, the dominant strategies for both firms are to play Strategy A and the outlined cell is the Nash equilibrium. If both firms play Strategy B then their payouts are greater ($2,325 each). Suppose that the firms collude and agree to play Strategy B. The dilemma is whether each firm can trust the other to play Strategy B and NOT Strategy A. Without a commitment device, each firm has an incentive to cheat to gain greater profit. The likely outcome is that they will both cheat and end up in the original Nash equilibrium.

The subject of **cartel** formation often arises when discussing oligopoly behavior. If the firms within the industry collude and successfully coordinate their business decisions, then a cartel is formed. A cartel acts like a monopoly as it controls the price and output of the market. This situation is highly inefficient. Consumers lose and the cartel's profits rise. The Organization of the Petroleum Exporting Countries (OPEC) is an example of a cartel.

NB10. Factor Markets (Micro)

#1. How do the roles of businesses and households differ in factor markets?

In markets for economic resources, **businesses demand economic inputs** such as land, labor, capital, and entrepreneurship to manufacture goods and services. Businesses make rental payments for land, wages and salary payments for labor, interest payments for capital, and profits to the entrepreneur.

Households are responsible for supplying the scarce economic resources to businesses. When laborers are willing to invest more in human capital through education and training, wages tend to be greater than workers that do NOT invest in obtaining higher skills. Unskilled labor will earn less than skilled labor.

Land Rent and Economic Rent: We can think of rent paid for land as a surplus payment since it is fixed in nature. As the price of land increases, there is no way to provide any additional units of this limited economic resource. **Any resource payment that exceeds what it takes to employ the resource is known as economic rent.** A popular example is a professional athlete who earns $10 million per season. It is very likely that this athlete would play for less than $10 million. If the athlete would accept $1 million for the season, his or her economic rent would equal $9 million. Because the athlete's talents are so scarce, the economic rent is very high.

#2. How do you calculate the marginal revenue product of an economic resource?

The demand for an economic resource is derived from the demand for goods and services. The **derived demand** for an economic resource is a firm's **marginal revenue product (MRP)**, the additional revenue a business receives from hiring one more unit of a resource. When you multiply the marginal revenue of a good (price in a perfectly competitive product market) by the marginal product of the resource, you get the marginal revenue product. Sometimes marginal product is called marginal *physical* product – don't let that confuse you.

$$MRP = MP \times MR$$

You can also take the change in total revenue and divide it by the change in number of economic inputs:

$$MRP = \frac{\Delta \text{Total Revenue}}{\Delta Q \text{ of Resources}}$$

#3. What are the determinants of marginal revenue product?

The determinants of marginal revenue product are the shift factors of the downward-sloping resource demand curve. Here are the three key determinants:

1. **Product price and demand** – If there is an increase in product demand, then there is more demand for the economic inputs used to make the product.
2. **Productivity of the resource** – If a resource is more productive, the firm wants to employ more (NOT less) of those productive resources to maximize profit. **An increase in productivity will also shift the marginal product curve upward.**
3. **Prices of substitute resources** – If the price of a substitute resource decreases, then there will be less demand for the other resource.

#4. How do you determine a firm's profit-maximizing quantity of an economic resource?

It is profitable for a firm to employ a resource as long as the marginal revenue product is greater than or equal to the **marginal factor cost** (MFC). The MFC is the additional cost of employing one more unit of a resource.

$$MRP = MFC$$

It is also acceptable to refer to MFC as marginal resource cost. In a perfectly competitive resource market, the MFC is equal to the price of the economic resource. **Therefore, in a perfectly competitive labor market the firm's MFC is the wage rate and the firm's supply of labor.** However, this is NOT true in an imperfectly competitive resource market.

#5. How do you illustrate a perfectly competitive labor market and firm using side-by-side graphs?

When graphing perfectly competitive resource markets such as labor, it is a good idea to graph the market for the resource and the firm hiring the resource side-by-side. The resource market sets the equilibrium price of the resource (wage rate) and the firm takes the price of the resource from the market. The firm is a "wage taker."

The resource market consists of a downward sloping demand curve representing the marginal revenue product, and an upward sloping supply curve.

Since the firm is a "wage taker," the firm's supply curve is perfectly elastic. This represents the firm's marginal factor cost. The firm's demand curve is a downward sloping marginal revenue product curve.

The following diagram illustrates a perfectly competitive firm hiring its labor (right) from a perfectly competitive labor market (left).

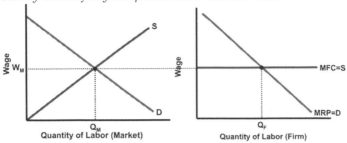

Side-By-Side Perfectly Competitive Labor Market & Firm

#6. How do changes in labor productivity affect wages and quantity of workers hired?

An increase in the productivity of labor will increase the marginal product of labor (MP_L) and the marginal revenue product of labor (MRP_L). This shifts the demand for labor to the right and increases the profit-maximizing quantity of workers to hire.

If all firms use new technology that increases the productivity of labor, the market demand for labor will increase and wages will rise.

If only one firm uses the new technology, then only the firm's demand for labor will shift to the right and wages will stay the same.

#7. How does a monopsonistic resource market compare to a perfectly competitive resource market?

A **monopsony** occurs when there is only one buyer of an economic resource. This is different from a monopoly, which has only one seller of a product.

If a firm has a monopsony in the labor market, it becomes a "wage maker." Its marginal factor cost curve lies above the labor supply curve and will hire labor where the MRP=MFC. However, it will pay its workers the lowest possible wage, which falls on the supply curve. The following graph illustrates a monopsony hiring its profit-maximizing number of workers.

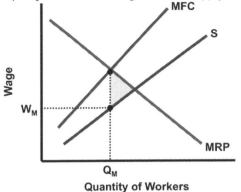

Monopsony: MRP=MFC, Wage on Labor Supply Curve

The shaded triangle above represents the deadweight loss resulting from monopsonistic conditions. If this were a perfectly competitive labor market, supply would equal the MRP. This results in higher wages and more workers hired than in a monopsony.

#8. How do you calculate the cost-minimizing combination of economic resources?

When a firm employs two types of resources, we can determine the cost-minimizing quantity of each input by using the marginal products and prices of each input. Here is the equation:

$$\frac{MP_{Labor}}{P_{Labor}} = \frac{MP_{Capital}}{P_{Capital}}$$

The ratios must equal one another. If you need MP/P to decrease, then hire more units of that resource. This is because of diminishing marginal returns (as additional inputs are hired, marginal product will decrease).

If you need MP/P to increase, then hire fewer units of that resource.

Note: This equation works similar to the consumer equilibrium formula in NB7, except here we are buying resources instead of goods and services.

#9. How do you calculate the profit-maximizing combination of economic resources?

When a firm employs two types of resources, we can determine the profit-maximizing quantity of each input by using the marginal revenue product of each input and the price of each input. Here is the equation:

$$\frac{MRP_{Labor}}{P_{Labor}} = \frac{MRP_{Capital}}{P_{Capital}} = 1$$

The ratios must be equal to one. If you need MRP/P to decrease, then hire more units of that resource. This is because of the law of diminishing marginal returns (as additional inputs are hired, marginal product and marginal revenue product will decrease).

If you need MRP/P to increase, then hire fewer units of that resource.

#10. What are the effects of union behavior in labor markets?

The main goal of a union is to raise the wages of its members. Here are several ways unions attempt to increase wages:

1. **Increase labor demand** – Unions can attempt to increase the demand for the goods it produces to raise the demand for workers. This can be done through advertising campaigns or lobbying the government for more spending on its products. A union can also attempt to raise the productivity of its members to increase the demand for labor.

2. **Decrease labor supply** – Union membership can depend on college degrees, certifications, and

licensing. By raising standards of its workers or increasing the difficulty of membership, the union can reduce the supply of workers to raise wages. This is sometimes referred to as an exclusive or craft union model.

3. **Commandeering the supply curve** – Union members can agree to strike when the wage rate falls below a union-determined level above the market equilibrium. This is similar to an effective **minimum wage** (or price floor) set by the government, which results in a surplus of labor in the labor market. Another name for this union model is the inclusive or industrial model.

NB11. The Government (Micro)

#1. What is the government's role within the economy?

The government serves many economic purposes. First, it is responsible for providing laws that **promote competitive behavior in product and factor markets**. The government establishes the rules of the game and passes antitrust laws. It ensures that property rights are protected and, when possible, clearly defined.

The government provides public goods and services and imposes taxes on businesses and households. It enacts appropriate fiscal policies (NB3), corrects market failures, and pursues actions that maintain free and fair international trade. The actions listed so far mostly represent the idealized role of the government.

Here are some actions of the government that do NOT generally increase economic efficiency:

1. **Minimum wages (price floors)** to help low-income sellers of labor artificially raise the costs of producing goods. This also leads to a **surplus** ($Q_S > Q_D$) of labor and creates deadweight loss.

Labor Market: Minimum Wage (Wage Floor) Effects

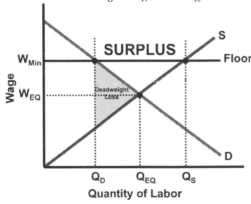

2. **Rent controls (price ceilings)** to help low-income

buyers artificially lower prices. This leads to a **shortage** ($Q_D > Q_S$) of housing and creates deadweight loss. In the long run, this can spur underground market activity and cause sellers to leave the industry.

Rental Market: Rent Control (Price Ceiling) Effects

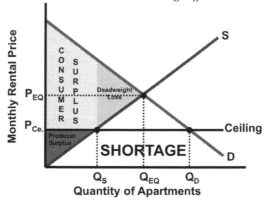

3. **Protective tariffs** artificially raise the prices of imports while protecting less efficient domestic industries. This also leads to deadweight loss.

Effects of a Per-Unit Protective Tariff

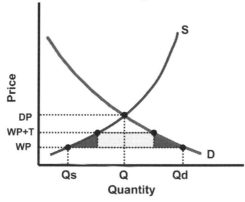

DP represents the domestic price, *WP* represents the world price, and *WP+T* represents the world price with the tariff. The shaded rectangle is the total tariff revenue collected by the government, and the two shaded triangles represent the deadweight loss created by the tariff. *Note: This graph is also referenced in NB6.*

#2. What are the characteristics of a public good?

One of the functions of government is to provide public goods such as national defense, roads, and streetlights. There are two characteristics of a public good:

1. **Shared consumption (non-rivalrous)** – One person's use of a public good does not prevent someone else from consuming it.
2. **Non-exclusion** – You cannot prevent people from enjoying the benefits of a public good.

The government provides public goods because the private sector will under produce these goods due to the **free-rider problem.** This occurs when we cannot restrict the consumption of a good so only paying customers receive the benefits. For example, it can be difficult to prevent nonpaying citizens from enjoying the benefits of clean air or flood control.

Another reason the government might provide a public good is because there might be **positive externalities**, or societal benefits, associated with the good. For example, education is a contributing factor to economic growth and higher living standards. Your neighbor is better off as a result of you becoming a well-educated citizen and contributing member of society. The ideal amount of a public good occurs where the marginal social cost is equal to the marginal social benefit.

#3. How do you graph a positive externality?

An externality occurs when a third party, someone other than the buyer or seller, is affected by a market transaction. This is known as a **market failure**. Externalities can be positive or negative.

A positive externality occurs when the marginal social benefit (MSB) of a good is greater than the marginal social cost (MSC). In other words, society is benefitting from the production of this good. This causes a misallocation of economic resources and deadweight loss. The market will under produce goods–such as education and flu vaccines–that generate positive externalities.

The graph below illustrates positive externalities (MSB>MSC). The area of deadweight loss is the shaded triangle. The equilibrium of P_1 and Q_1 is socially optimal, however the market generates a price of P and quantity of Q. Society is getting too little of the good at too low of a price.

Product Market with Positive Externalities: MSB>MSC

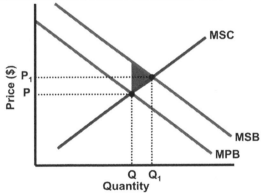

#4. How do you graph a negative externality?

A **negative externality** occurs when the marginal social cost (MSC) of a good is greater than the marginal social benefit (MSB). Society is worse off from the production of the good. There is a misallocation of economic resources and deadweight loss. Private markets overproduce goods–such as cigarettes and alcohol–that generate negative externalities.

The next graph illustrates a good that creates negative externalities (MSC>MSB). The area of deadweight loss is the shaded triangle. The equilibrium of P_1 and Q_1 is socially optimal, however the market generates a price of P and quantity of Q. Society is getting too much of the good at too low of a price.

Product Market with Negative Externalities: MSC>MSB

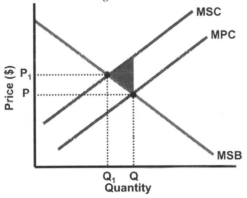

#5. How can the government correct positive and negative externalities?

The government can correct a positive externality by offering buyers per-unit subsidies or incentives to increase demand so that the MSB=MSC. Another policy option is to offer sellers **per-unit subsidies** (Pigovian subsidy) to encourage more production so the MSB=MSC. These policy actions will get rid of the deadweight loss in the market if the per-unit subsidies equal the per-unit externalities.

The government can correct a negative externality by imposing **per-unit taxes on producers** (Pigovian tax) to raise the costs of production. This will shift supply left so the MSC=MSB. Another policy option is to tax buyers so that the MSC=MSB. In the end, the correction will eliminate deadweight loss from the market if the per-unit taxes equal the per-unit externalities.

A **government failure** can occur if the government action worsens deadweight loss in a market. For example, if the government increases per-unit taxes on the production of a good that creates positive externalities, the deadweight loss will increase and society is worse off.

#6. What are the principles that govern taxation?

Taxes are necessary because they provide revenue for the government to function and provide public goods. There are two principles of taxation:
1. **Ability-to-pay principle** – People should be taxed based on what they can afford. An example is a progressive income tax.
2. **Benefits-received principle** – People should be taxed based on what they get in return. An **excise tax** is a tax on a specific good. Revenue from a gasoline tax can be put toward maintaining roads, which would benefit the taxpaying drivers.

#7. How do the three types of taxes differ?

There are three types of taxes:
1. **Progressive tax** – A greater proportion of income is paid by those with higher levels of income than those with lower levels of income. An example is the federal income tax.
2. **Regressive tax** – A greater proportion of income is paid by those with lower levels of income than

those with higher levels of income. An example is a state sales tax.
3. **Proportional tax** – The proportion of one's income taxed is constant at all income levels. An example is the 10% tithe paid to the church in medieval Europe.

#8. What are the effects of a per-unit tax?

When the government imposes a per-unit tax, marginal costs increase and the supply curve shifts to the left. The producer and consumer both share part of the tax burden. As a result of the tax, the producer surplus and consumer surplus decrease. **Assuming there are no externalities, a per-unit tax will create deadweight loss.**

Effects of a Per-Unit Tax

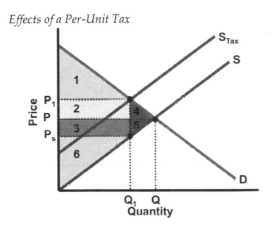

The diagram above illustrates the effects of a per-unit tax. P represents price before the tax, P_1 is the price after the tax, and P_s is the price the seller receives.

The shaded rectangle labeled 2 represents the portion of the tax that the buyer pays to the government, while 3 represents the portion of the tax that the seller pays to the government. These two shaded rectangles make up the total tax revenue, which can be calculated as $(P_1 - P_s) \times Q_1$. The shaded triangles labeled 4 and 5 make up the area of deadweight loss.

Consumer surplus before the tax consists of the areas of *1*, *2*, and *4*. After the tax, the consumer surplus only includes *1*. The producer surplus before the tax is *3*, *5*, and *6*. After the tax, producer surplus shrinks down to the triangle represented by *6*.

#9. How does the elasticity of demand and supply affect tax incidence?

Consumers and producers share the burden of a per-unit tax. In the previous example, the buyers and sellers share the tax burden equally since the elasticity of the demand curve and the elasticity of the supply curve are the same. When the elasticity of one curve is different, the tax burden is no longer equal. The incidence of the tax will fall more heavily on either the buyer or the seller. You can compare the tax burdens in the following examples by taking note of each curve's relative elasticity and by looking at the shaded rectangles.

If the demand curve is more elastic (flatter) than the supply curve, sellers will pay most of the tax. This is because consumers are more responsive to the increase in price caused by the tax.

Per-Unit Tax: Demand More Elastic Than Supply

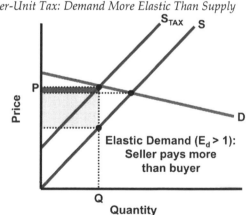

If the supply curve is more elastic than the demand curve, buyers will pay most of the tax. This is because

100

consumers are less responsive to the increase in price caused by the tax when demand is inelastic.

Per-Unit Tax: Supply More Elastic Than Demand

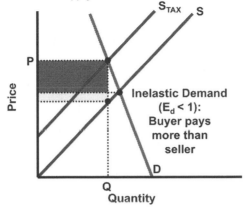

If the demand curve is perfectly elastic (horizontal), the sellers will pay all of the tax. This is because consumers are completely responsive to any increase in price.

Per-Unit Tax: Perfectly Elastic Demand Curve

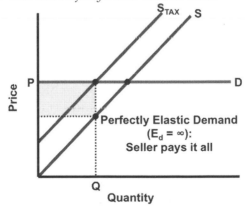

If the demand curve is perfectly inelastic (vertical), the buyers will pay all of the tax. This is because consumers are completely unresponsive to the higher price brought on by the tax.

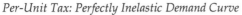
Per-Unit Tax: Perfectly Inelastic Demand Curve

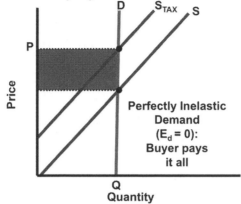

#10. How does the government attempt to reduce income inequality?

Another function of the government in a mixed market economy is to reduce income inequality within the nation. A **Lorenz curve** shows the amount of income inequality in a given economy. In theory, the government can shift the Lorenz curve inward toward greater equality (45° line) through progressive tax systems and transfer programs such as welfare payments that support low-income households. While these actions can lessen income inequality, these actions can also lead to the misallocation of resources and cause greater inefficiencies.

Lorenz Curve: Income Inequality

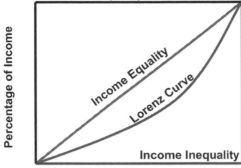

No Bull Review Sheet – Microeconomics

Top 10 Microeconomics Concepts to Know

1. Shift factors of demand (tastes, income, #buyers, price expectations, substitute prices, complement prices) & supply (resource prices, tech, productivity, production taxes, subsidies, price expectations, alternative output prices), *NB1*
2. Effects of price floors (above equilibrium-surpluses) & ceilings (below equilibrium-shortages), *NB1, NB11*
3. Elasticity – elastic demand when P & TR move opposite ways, MR is positive; inelastic demand when P & TR move same way, MR is negative, *NB7*
4. Diminishing marginal returns – hire additional labor, additional output falls; explains relationships of cost curves, *NB8*
5. Perfect competition – SR profits cause more firms to enter market in long run causing firm to break even (highly efficient), *NB9*
6. Monopoly – P>MC so inefficient; P=MC socially optimal; P=ATC fair return, MR=0 TR maximization, *NB9*
7. Effects of Per-Unit & Lump-Sum Taxes & Subsidies: per-unit shifts MC, changes output & profits; lump-sum does NOT shift MC, changes profits, *NB8, NB11*
8. Game Theory – firm plays dominant strategy, best strategy regardless of other firm's decision; find Nash equilibrium , *NB9*
9. Positive externalities (MSB>MSC) corrected by per-unit subsidies & negative externalities (MSC>MSB) corrected by per-unit taxes, *NB11*
10. Tax incidence & elasticity – more elastic demand means seller pays more; more inelastic demand means buyer pays more, *NB11*

Top 5 Microeconomics Models to Master

1. Supply & Demand Graphs, *NB1*
2. Perfectly Competitive Market & Firm Graphs, *NB9*
3. Monopoly Graphs, *NB9*
4. Perfectly Competitive Factor Market & Firm Graphs, *NB10*
5. Positive & Negative Externality Graphs, *NB11*

Other important models for Microeconomics:
Production Possibilities Graphs, *NB1*
Monopolistic Competition Graphs, NB9
Per-Unit Tax Graphs, *NB11*

Top 5 Microeconomics Formulas to Master
1. Utility-Maximizing Combination, *NB7*
2. Price Elasticity of Demand & Total Revenue Test, *NB7*
3. Marginal Product & Average Product, *NB8*
4. Per-Unit Costs & Marginal Cost, *NB8*
5. Resource Combos (Cost-Minimizing & Profit-Max), *NB10*

Other important formulas for Microeconomics:
Income Elasticity, *NB7*
Cross-Price Elasticity, *NB7*
Supply Elasticity, *NB7*

Ready for practice questions and worksheets?
Check out *No Bull Review – For Use with the AP Macroeconomics & AP Microeconomics Exams* full-size review book.

Free review videos available at **www.MrMedico.info** and www.youtube.com/user/medicotube

Thank you for choosing **No Bull Review** for your studying and test prep needs. We hope you found the No Bull Approach helpful and effective.

Good Luck!

Index

110

39858947R00065

Made in the USA
Lexington, KY
15 March 2015